MW00716661

Aug 30/2003.

Dear Shirley,

I hope you will always remember,
Shirley, I loved my brother, Arne,
very much. I was proud to call
him my brother, what he accomplished
in Mexico, in the last 10 years
of his life was amazing, That
is now his living legazy, a memory
that hopefully will go on.
I want to regain our family bond,
Prayers = Love, Gunni.

© 2002 by Barbour Publishing, Inc.

ISBN 1-58660-441-4

All rights reserved. No part of this publication may be reproduced or transmitted in any form or by any means without written permission of the publisher.

Cover art © Images.com

Selections on pages 20, 22, 30, and 32 are by Viola Ruelke Gommer and are used with the author's permission. Selections by Eldyn Simons are taken from *The Dawn of Hope: Encouragement for Those Who Grieve* (Barbour Publishing, 2000).

Scripture quotations marked NLT are taken from the *Holy Bible,* New Living Translation, copyright © 1996. Used by permission of Tyndale House Publishers, Inc. Wheaton, Illinois 60189, U.S.A. All rights reserved.

Scripture quotations marked NIV are taken from the HOLY BIBLE, NEW INTERNATIONAL VERSION®. NIV®. Copyright © 1973, 1978, 1984 by International Bible Society. Used by permission of Zondervan Publishing House. All rights reserved.

Scripture quotations marked NRSV are taken from the New Revised Standard Version Bible, copyright 1989, Division of Christian Education of the National Council of the Churches of Christ in the United States of America. Used by permission. All rights reserved.

Scripture quotations marked TLB are taken from *The Living Bible* copyright © 1971. Used by permission of Tyndale House Publishers, Inc., Wheaton, Illinois 60189. All rights reserved.

Published by Barbour Books, an imprint of Barbour Publishing, Inc.,
P.O. Box 719, Uhrichsville, Ohio 44683
www.barbourbooks.com

Member of the
Evangelical Christian
Publishers Association

Printed in China.

In Your Time of Loss

Ellyn Sanna

My prayers and thoughts are with you during this difficult time. . . .

CONTENTS

In God's Hands 7
The Gift of Memory 11
God's Peace 15
The Comfort of His Presence 19
Count on Me 27
Going Home 33

Blessed are
those who mourn,
for they will be comforted.

MATTHEW 5:4 NIV

1

In God's Hands

That which I have placed in God's hands
I still have.

MARTIN LUTHER

I know how much it hurts to let go of someone you love. But nothing we surrender to God is really lost. My words cannot take away your pain and loneliness, your longing for that one beloved face—but I promise you:

Through Christ,
your loved one is safe with God.

Your [loved] ones are in good hands.
God is keeping them safe until the Dawn. . .
waiting for you to hold them once again in your arms.

ELDYN SIMONS

*Have you not put a hedge around him
and his household
and everything he has?*

JOB 1:10 NIV

God has put a "hedge" around your life. That hedge is the love of Christ—and even death cannot knock it down. Enclosed by His eternal compassion and tender care, your life and your loved ones are forever protected from harm. Death may cast its dark shadow over your life—but shadows have no power to rob our eternal safety. One day, you and your loved one will once more walk—together—in the bright light of God's heavenly presence.

There is nothing we can lose on earth
that can rob us of the treasures
God has given us and will give us.

JOHN OXENHAM

*Anything good you've ever been given
is yours forever.*

RACHEL NAOMI REMEN

I know the one in whom I trust,
and I am sure that he is able to guard
what I have entrusted to him
until the day of his return.

2 TIMOTHY 1:12 NLT

2

The Gift of Memory

The memory of the righteous will be a blessing.

<small>PROVERBS 10:7 NIV</small>

"*All* that's left are the memories," we sometimes say, as though memories were mere intangible wisps of fancy. But memories are more than that. They are a gift from God, reminding us that Time is not the final victor. Just as your loved one will live forever in your heart and mind, so that person will live eternally in Christ.

Your memories are not a delusion. They are a glimpse of a reality far more solid and lasting than this world will ever offer. Take comfort in them. Those we love may be separated from us by death—but nothing can ever take them from our hearts.

The memory of your dear [one], instead of an agony,
will yet be a sad sweet feeling in your heart,
of a purer, and holier sort than you have known before.

ABRAHAM LINCOLN

*He who has gone,
so we but cherish his memory, abides with us,
more potent, nay, more present,
than the living man.*

ANTOINE DE SAINT-EXUPÉRY

Memory heals and encourages us to face the future.
Memory does not ignore the fact that our loved one is dead,
but it does give us a continuing hold on that beloved life.
Properly used, memory can lift us above the finality of death.

ELDYN SIMONS

The cares and interests hold familiar places
in our lives and hearts again,
in part because those we love helped us
to make room for them there.

THOMAS ATTIC

Sometimes it may seem as though everywhere you turn you're pierced by new reminders of your loss. Familiar places, common activities, even the ordinary daily routines of your life are filled with the constant, painful awareness that the person you love is missing.

But life's beauties and comforts have not been destroyed forever by your loss. The very dearness of these places and activities were in part created by your loved one's presence. They are gifts from that beloved person—gifts that you will one day take up and enjoy once again. You can treasure them still more, knowing that they tie you to the one who is gone.

3

God's Peace

You will keep in perfect peace all who trust in you,
whose thoughts are fixed on you!

ISAIAH 26:3 NLT

Comfort is the touch of God when we thought we were alone in the darkness. It is the promise that the dawn is on its way.

ELDYN SIMONS

Ultimately, your deepest and most lasting healing can only be found in God. Those of us who love you will do whatever we can to help—but only God can give your heart peace.

I am learning from experience that there is a deep peace that grows out of. . .loneliness. . . . These things do drive me up my hill to God, and then there comes into my soul through the very tears a comfort which is so much better than laughter.

FRANK LAUBACH

As a mother comforts her child,
so I will comfort you.

ISAIAH 66:13 NIV

Grief is a long, slow journey. Its path has many twists and turns; you may spend time in dark narrow alleys or dismal cul-de-sacs, long barren stretches of empty highway or exhausting mountain roads. Each person's journey along this path will be different; and there are no shortcuts.

Give yourself time. Be patient with the demands of this difficult journey. Rely on God's peace to ease your mind and help you heal.

What wound did ever heal but by degrees?

SHAKESPEARE

4

The Comfort of His Presence

The LORD is close to the brokenhearted
and saves those who are crushed in spirit.

PSALM 34:18 NIV

We can rejoice, too, when we run into problems and trials, for we know that they are good for us—they help us learn to endure. And endurance develops strength of character in us, and character strengthens our confident expectation of salvation. And this expectation will not disappoint us. For we know how dearly God loves us, because he has given us the Holy Spirit to fill our hearts with his love.

ROMANS 5:3–5 NLT

Verses like these sometimes seem like poor comfort. But that's because we often misinterpret them. We think that we should take consolation in learning endurance, when really the endurance and strength of character are just byproducts from the true source of comfort—the Holy Spirit's presence in our hearts. He alone will give us the certainty that we are loved. And with His assurance, we have hope. We can be confident that our loved ones and ourselves are safe for all eternity. We have the Spirit's guarantee.

Now it is God who. . .
has given us the Spirit as a deposit,
guaranteeing what is to come.

2 CORINTHIANS 5:5 NIV

You are not alone.
God is with you during this difficult time.
He has not abandoned you.
And many prayers are offered up for you,
asking that you will receive
unfaltering trust,
courage, and
most of all God's peace.

May your unfailing love be my comfort.

PSALM 119:76 NIV

$\mathcal{H}$e lifted me out of the pit of despair,
out of the mud and the mire.
He set my feet on solid ground
and steadied me as I walked along.
He has given me a new song to sing. . . .

PSALM 40:2–3 NLT

Though we stumble,
we shall not fall headlong,
for the L ORD holds us by the hand.

PSALM 37:24 NRSV

For I am convinced that neither death nor life,
neither angels nor demons,
neither the present nor the future,
nor any powers, neither height nor depth,
nor anything else in all creation,
will be able to separate us from the love of God
that is in Christ Jesus our Lord.

ROMANS 8:38–39 NIV

A door has closed in your life.
You cannot open it again.
But God walked through that door with you.
He is here with you in this sad, cold place.
Stop looking at that shut door.
The sight will only break your heart.
Turn around now.
Look toward the future.
It may look dark and unknown.
But it is not unknown to God,
and He will walk with you all the way.

I think these difficult times have helped me
to understand better than before how infinitely rich
and beautiful life is in every way and that
so many things that one goes around worrying about
are of no importance whatsoever.

ISAK DINESEN

During times like these, we see life and God in a new way. At first, this new vision may seem too painful to bear. . . but slowly, you will come to look at life from a new perspective. The truly essential things will stand out, while the trivial things that once occupied your attention no longer seem so important. As you sit in the dark, look up—and see how bright the stars are shining.

*When it is dark enough,
you can see the stars.*

CHARLES BEARD

5

Count on Me

Together we'll share it,
Together we'll bear it,
Together we'll see it through.

RUTH ALLA WAGER

The first duty of love is to listen.

PAUL TILLICH

There's so little I can do to help. I can't lift this terrible load you're carrying. I don't know how to make you smile again.

But I *can* listen, whenever you want to talk. And I'm always here if you need me.

Don't try to carry this burden all by yourself. Don't feel as though you have to be strong and never let anyone know how much you're hurting. Share your pain with those of us who love you.

He who conceals his grief
finds no remedy for it.

OLD TURKISH PROVERB

Give sorrow words: the grief that does not speak
Whispers the o'er fraught heart, and bids it break.

SHAKESPEARE

You can't heal a wound
by saying it's not there!

JEREMIAH 6:14 TLB

I wish I could take your pain and loss away.
I can't.
All I can do is cry with you
and hold you up in prayer.
Please know I am always available. . .
an ear to listen, a shoulder on which to cry. . .
whatever I can do to help,
anything at all,
please let me know.
We will stand together against the pain.
I will walk with you through this dark valley of grief,
no matter how long it takes
until you see the sun again.
You are not alone.

The loss of a loved one makes us
feel frightened and alone—
but love can build a hedge around our hearts,
a shelter of continuing strength.
If you are hurting. . .
allow others to give you the shelter of comfort—
and then reach out yourself to help build
a hedge of love around another's heart.

ELDYN SIMONS

When I was hurting, you were there for me. Now let me do the same for you. I know that down the road you will pass on any strength you find to someone else in need.

Together we form a chain of love. We need each other.

You are in a dark, desolate place
where you find it hard to pray.
Words will not come.
You feel no hope, no joy, no confidence.
All promises seem shattered
and everything is dark.

I know that dark, sad place,
for I have been there too.
But God has led me into the light.
I can see the way ahead.
Lean on me.
I will lend you my strength when
you are too weak to walk.
I will offer up prayers of petition and praise,
when you cannot find the words.
I will be your eyes when yours are
too filled with tears to see.
Count on me.

6

Going Home

There are many rooms in my Father's home,
and I am going to prepare a place for you. . . .
When everything is ready, I will come and get you. . . .

JESUS (JOHN 14:2–3 NLT)

This world is not our permanent residence.
One day we will all go home—
and then we will be together forever.

After the resurrection the apostles never used the word death to express the close of a Christian's earthly life. They referred to the passing of a Christian as "at home with the Lord," "to depart and be with Jesus.". . .

JOHN M. DRESCHER

The LORD will be your everlasting light,
and your days of sorrow will end.

ISAIAH 60:20 NIV

It's so hard to understand why things happen the way they do. *Why?* our hearts cry. *Why does it have to be this way?* It just doesn't seem right that our loved one should leave us. Everything inside our hearts cries out in rebellion against death.

Death *is* unnatural. It's not the way God meant things to be. Our hearts were designed for eternity. And one day, in heaven, we will no longer ask *Why?*

I shall know why—
when Time is over—
And I have ceased to wonder why—
Christ will explain each separate anguish
in the fair schoolroom in the sky.

EMILY DICKINSON

In the midst of winter,
I finally learned there was in me
an invincible summer.

ALBERT CAMUS

Summer is a time of life and growth—but in the winter everything dies. Right now your heart may be so frozen with grief that you think summer will never come again.

But even in the bleakest, coldest winters, life waits beneath the snow. And you too will find the life of God's Spirit stirring in your heart. No winter blizzard, no freezing rain can kill the eternal life He brings.

Heaven's summer is where your heart belongs.

The soul that rises with us, our life's star,
Hath had elsewhere its setting,
And cometh from afar. . . .
Trailing clouds of glory, do we come
From God, who is our home.

WILLIAM WORDSWORTH

Is death the last step?
No, it is the final awakening.

SIR WALTER SCOTT

And can it be that. . .the loss of one. . .
makes a void in my heart,
so wide and deep that nothing
but the width and depth of eternity
can fill it up!

CHARLES DICKENS

This world can never offer total comfort
for the pain you feel.
Only heaven can.

All those glorious sunrises that God in His love
gave this world will pale before the wondrous beauty
and pageantry of that Day that will fulfill
all the hopes and promises of the ages.
We shall see our Lord face-to-face.
In that Day, we will truly come into the light.
The sorrows and pains of this life will forever be forgotten;
all the broken hearts shall be made whole. . . .
Our great enemy, death, shall be no more.

ELDYN SIMONS

*God washes the eyes with tears
until they can behold the invisible land
where tears shall be no more.*

HENRY WARD BEECHER

I am so sorry for your loss.
I pray that you will find comfort
in the promises of God.
May you know His peace even now.